Original Short Stories of Maupassant

Vol. 12

Guy de Maupassant

CONTENTS

THE CHILD

A COUNTRY EXCURSION

ROSE

ROSALIE PRUDENT

REGRET

A SISTER'S CONFESSION

COCO

DEAD WOMAN'S SECRET

A HUMBLE DRAMA

MADEMOISELLE COCOTTE

THE CORSICAN BANDIT

THE GRAVE

THE CHILD

Lemonnier had remained a widower with one child. He had loved his wife devotedly, with a tender and exalted love, without a slip, during their entire married life. He was a good, honest man, perfectly simple, sincere, without suspicion or malice.

He fell in love with a poor neighbor, proposed and was accepted. He was making a very comfortable living out of the wholesale cloth business, and he did not for a minute suspect that the young girl might have accepted him for anything else but himself.

She made him happy. She was everything to him; he only thought of her, looked at her continually, with worshiping eyes. During meals he would make any number of blunders, in order not to have to take his eyes from the beloved face; he would pour the wine in his plate and the water in the salt-cellar, then he would laugh like a child, repeating:

"You see, I love you too much; that makes me crazy."

She would smile with a calm and resigned look; then she would look away, as though embarrassed by the adoration of her husband, and try to make him talk about something else; but he would take her hand under the table and he would hold it in his, whispering:

"My little Jeanne, my darling little Jeanne!"

She sometimes lost patience and said:

"Come, come, be reasonable; eat and let me eat."

He would sigh and break off a mouthful of bread, which he would then chew slowly.

For five years they had no children. Then suddenly she announced to him that this state of affairs would soon cease. He was wild with joy. He no longer left her for a minute, until his old nurse, who had brought him up and who often ruled the house, would push him out and close the door behind him, in order to compel him to go out in the fresh air.

He had grown very intimate with a young man who had known his wife since childhood, and who was one of the prefect's secretaries. M. Duretour would dine three times a week with the Lemonniers, bringing flowers to madame, and sometimes a box at the theater; and often, at the end of the dinner, Lemonnier, growing tender, turning towards his wife, would explain: "With a companion like you and a friend like him, a man is completely happy on earth."

She died in childbirth. The shock almost killed him. But the sight of the child, a poor, moaning little creature, gave him courage.

He loved it with a passionate and sorrowful love, with a morbid love in which stuck the memory of death, but in which lived something of his worship for the dead mother. It was the flesh of his wife, her being continued, a sort of quintessence of herself. This child was her very life transferred to another body; she had disappeared that it might exist, and the father would smother it in with kisses. But also, this child had killed her; he had stolen this beloved creature, his life was at the cost of hers. And M. Lemonnier would place his son in the cradle and would sit down and watch him. He would sit this way by the hour, looking at him, dreaming of thousands of things, sweet or sad. Then, when the little one was asleep, he would bend over him and sob.

The child grew. The father could no longer spend an hour away from him; he would stay near him, take him out for walks, and himself dress him, wash him, make him eat. His friend, M. Duretour, also seemed to love the boy; he would kiss him wildly, in those frenzies of tenderness which are characteristic of parents. He would toss him in his arms, he would trot him on his knees, by the hour, and M. Lemonnier, delighted, would mutter:

"Isn't he a darling? Isn't he a darling?"

And M. Duretour would hug the child in his arms and tickle his neck with his mustache.

Celeste, the old nurse, alone, seemed to have no tenderness for the little one. She would grow angry at his pranks, and seemed impatient at the caresses of the two men. She would exclaim:

"How can you expect to bring a child up like that? You'll make a perfect monkey out of him."

Years went by, and Jean was nine years old. He hardly knew how to read; he had been so spoiled, and only did as he saw fit. He was willful, stubborn and quick-tempered. The father always gave in to him and let him have his own way. M. Duretour would always buy him all the toys he wished, and he fed him on cake and candies. Then Celeste would grow angry and exclaim:

"It's a shame, monsieur, a shame. You are spoiling this child. But it will have to stop; yes, sir, I tell you it will have to stop, and before long, too."

M. Lemonnier would answer, smiling:

"What can you expect? I love him too much, I can't resist him; you must get used to it."

Jean was delicate, rather. The doctor said that he was anaemic, prescribed iron, rare meat and broth.

But the little fellow loved only cake and refused all other nourishment; and the father, in despair, stuffed him with cream-puffs and chocolate eclairs.

One evening, as they were sitting down to supper, Celeste brought on the soup with an air of authority and an assurance which she did not usually have. She took off the cover and, dipping the ladle into the dish, she declared:

"Here is some broth such as I have never made; the young one will have to take some this time."

M. Lemonnier, frightened, bent his head. He saw a storm brewing.

Celeste took his plate, filled it herself and placed it in front of him.

He tasted the soup and said:

"It is, indeed, excellent."

The servant took the boy's plate and poured a spoonful of soup in it. Then she retreated a few steps and waited.

Jean smelled the food and pushed his plate away with an expression of disgust. Celeste, suddenly pale, quickly stepped forward and forcibly poured a spoonful down the child's open mouth.

He choked, coughed, sneezed, spat; howling, he seized his glass and threw it at his nurse. She received it full in the stomach. Then, exasperated, she took the young shaver's head under her arm and began pouring spoonful after spoonful of soup down his throat. He grew as red as a beet, and he would cough it up, stamping, twisting, choking, beating the air with his hands.

At first the father was so surprised that he could not move. Then, suddenly, he rushed forward, wild with rage, seized the servant by the throat and threw her up against the wall stammering:

"Out! Out! Out! you brute!"

But she shook him off, and, her hair streaming down her back, her eyes snapping, she cried out:

"What's gettin' hold of you? You're trying to thrash me because I am making this child eat soup when you are filling him with sweet stuff!"

He kept repeating, trembling from head to foot:

"Out! Get out-get out, you brute!"

Then, wild, she turned to him and, pushing her face up against his, her voice trembling:

"Ah!—you think-you think that you can treat me like that? Oh! no. And for whom?—for that brat who is not even yours. No, not yours! No, not yours—not yours! Everybody knows it, except yourself! Ask the grocer, the butcher, the baker, all of them, any one of them!"

She was growling and mumbling, choked with passion; then she stopped and looked at him.

He was motionless livid, his arms hanging by his sides. After a short pause, he murmured in a faint, shaky voice, instinct with deep feeling:

"You say? you say? What do you say?"

She remained silent, frightened by his appearance. Once more he stepped forward, repeating:

"You say—what do you say?"

Then in a calm voice, she answered:

"I say what I know, what everybody knows."

He seized her and, with the fury of a beast, he tried to throw her down. But, although old, she was strong and nimble. She slipped under his arm, and running around the table once more furious, she screamed:

"Look at him, just look at him, fool that you are! Isn't he the living image of M. Durefour? just look at his nose and his eyes! Are yours like that? And his hair! Is it like his mother's? I tell you that everyone knows it, everyone except yourself! It's the joke of the town! Look at him!"

She went to the door, opened it, and disappeared.

Jean, frightened, sat motionless before his plate of soup.

At the end of an hour, she returned gently, to see how matters stood. The child, after doing away with all the cakes and a pitcher full of cream and one of syrup, was now emptying the jam-pot with his soup-spoon.

The father had gone out.

Celeste took the child, kissed him, and gently carried him to his room and put him to bed. She came back to the dining-room, cleared the table, put everything in place, feeling very uneasy all the time.

Not a single sound could be heard throughout the house. She put her ear against's her master's door. He seemed to be perfectly still. She put her eye to the keyhole. He was writing, and seemed very calm.

Then she returned to the kitchen and sat down, ready for any emergency. She slept on a chair and awoke at daylight.

She did the rooms as she had been accustomed to every morning; she swept and dusted, and, towards eight o'clock, prepared M. Lemonnier's breakfast.

But she did not dare bring it to her master, knowing too well how she would be received; she waited for him to ring. But he did not ring. Nine o'clock, then ten o'clock went by.

Celeste, not knowing what to think, prepared her tray and started up with it, her heart beating fast.

3

She stopped before the door and listened. Everything was still. She knocked; no answer. Then, gathering up all her courage, she opened the door and entered. With a wild shriek, she dropped the breakfast tray which she had been holding in her hand.

In the middle of the room, M. Lemonnier was hanging by a rope from a ring in the ceiling. His tongue was sticking out horribly. His right slipper was lying on the ground, his left one still on his foot. An upturned chair had rolled over to the bed.

Celeste, dazed, ran away shrieking. All the neighbors crowded together. The physician declared that he had died at about midnight.

A letter addressed to M. Duretdur was found on the table of the suicide. It contained these words:

"I leave and entrust the child to you!"

A COUNTRY EXCURSION

For five months they had been talking of going to take luncheon in one of the country suburbs of Paris on Madame Dufour's birthday, and as they were looking forward very impatiently to the outing, they rose very early that morning. Monsieur Dufour had borrowed the milkman's wagon and drove himself. It was a very tidy, two-wheeled conveyance, with a cover supported by four iron rods, with curtains that had been drawn up, except the one at the back, which floated out like a sail. Madame Dufour, resplendent in a wonderful, cherry colored silk dress, sat by the side of her husband.

The old grandmother and a girl sat behind them on two chairs, and a boy with yellow hair was lying at the bottom of the wagon, with nothing to be seen of him except his head.

When they reached the bridge of Neuilly, Monsieur Dufour said: "Here we are in the country at last!" and at that signal his wife grew sentimental about the beauties of nature. When they got to the crossroads at Courbevoie they were seized with admiration for the distant landscape. On the right was Argenteuil with its bell tower, and above it rose the hills of Sannois and the mill of Orgemont, while on the left the aqueduct of Marly stood out against the clear morning sky, and in the distance they could see the terrace of Saint-Germain; and opposite them, at the end of a low chain of hills, the new fort of Cormeilles. Quite in the distance; a very long way off, beyond the plains and village, one could see the sombre green of the forests.

The sun was beginning to burn their faces, the dust got into their eyes, and on either side of the road there stretched an interminable tract of bare, ugly country with an unpleasant odor. One might have thought that it had been ravaged by a pestilence, which had even attacked the buildings, for skeletons of dilapidated and deserted houses, or small cottages, which were left in an unfinished state, because the contractors had not been paid, reared their four roofless walls on each side.

Here and there tall factory chimneys rose up from the barren soil. The only vegetation on that putrid land, where the spring breezes wafted an odor of petroleum and slate, blended with another odor that was even less agreeable. At last, however, they crossed the Seine a second time, and the bridge was a delight. The river sparkled in the sun, and they had a feeling of quiet enjoyment, felt refreshed as they drank in the purer air that was not impregnated by the black smoke of factories nor by the miasma from the deposits of night soil. A man whom they met told them that the name of the place was Bezons. Monsieur Dufour pulled up and read the attractive announcement outside an eating house: Restaurant Poulin, matelottes and fried fish, private rooms, arbors, and swings.

"Well, Madame Dufour, will this suit you? Will you make up your mind at last?"

She read the announcement in her turn and then looked at the house for some time.

It was a white country inn, built by the roadside, and through the open door she could see the bright zinc of the counter, at which sat two workmen in their Sunday clothes. At last she made up her mind and said:

"Yes, this will do; and, besides, there is a view."

They drove into a large field behind the inn, separated from the river by the towing path, and dismounted. The husband sprang out first and then held out his arms for his wife, and as the step was very high Madame Dufour, in order to reach him, had to show the lower part of her limbs, whose former slenderness had disappeared in fat, and Monsieur Dufour, who was already getting excited by the country air, pinched her calf, and then, taking her in his arms, he set her on the ground, as if she had been some enormous bundle. She shook the dust out of the silk dress and then looked round to see in what sort of a place she was.

She was a stout woman, of about thirty-six, full-blown, and delightful to look at. She could hardly breathe, as her corsets were laced too tightly, and their pressure forced her superabundant bosom up to her double chin. Next the girl placed her hand on her father's shoulder and jumped down lightly. The boy with the yellow hair had got down by stepping on the wheel, and he helped Monsieur Dufour to lift his grandmother out. Then they unharnessed the horse, which they had tied to a tree, and the carriage fell back, with both shafts in the air. The men took off their coats and washed their hands in a pail of water and then went and joined the ladies, who had already taken possession of the swings.

Mademoiselle Dufour was trying to swing herself standing up, but she could not succeed in getting a start. She was a pretty girl of about eighteen, one of those women who suddenly excite your desire when you meet them in the street and who leave you with a vague feeling of uneasiness and of excited senses. She was tall, had a small waist and large hips, with a dark skin, very large eyes and very black hair. Her dress clearly marked the outlines of her firm, full figure, which was accentuated by the motion of her hips as she tried to swing herself higher. Her arms were stretched upward to hold the rope, so that her bosom rose at every movement she made. Her hat, which a gust of wind had blown off, was hanging behind her, and as the swing gradually rose higher and higher, she showed her delicate limbs up to the knees each time, and the breeze from her flying skirts, which was more heady than the fumes of wine, blew into the faces of the two men, who were looking at her and smiling.

Sitting in the other swing, Madame Dufour kept saying in a monotonous voice:

"Cyprian, come and swing me; do come and swing me, Cyprian!"

At last he went, and turning up his shirt sleeves, as if undertaking a hard piece of work, with much difficulty he set his wife in motion. She clutched the two ropes and held her legs out straight, so as not to touch the ground. She enjoyed feeling dizzy at the motion of the swing, and her whole figure shook like a jelly on a dish, but as she went higher and higher; she became too giddy and was frightened. Each time the swing came down she uttered a piercing scream, which made all the little urchins in the neighborhood come round, and down below, beneath the garden hedge, she vaguely saw a row of mischievous heads making various grimaces as they laughed.

When a servant girl came out they ordered luncheon.

"Some fried fish, a rabbit saute, salad and dessert," Madame Dufour said, with an important air.

"Bring two quarts of beer and a bottle of claret," her husband said.

"We will have lunch on the grass," the girl added.

The grandmother, who had an affection for cats, had been running after one that belonged to the house, trying to coax it to come to her for the last ten minutes. The animal, who was no doubt secretly flattered by her attentions, kept close to the good woman, but just out of reach of her hand, and quietly walked round the trees, against which she rubbed herself, with her tail up, purring with pleasure.

"Hello!" suddenly exclaimed the young man with the yellow hair, who was wandering about. "Here are two swell boats!" They all went to look at them and saw two beautiful canoes in a wooden shed; they were as beautifully finished as if they had been ornamental furniture. They hung side by side, like two tall, slender girls, in their narrow shining length, and made one wish to float in them on warm summer mornings and evenings along the flower-covered banks of the river, where the trees dip their branches into the water, where the rushes are continually rustling in the breeze and where the swift kingfishers dart about like flashes of blue lightning.

The whole family looked at them with great respect.

"Oh, they are indeed swell boats!" Monsieur Dufour repeated gravely, as he examined them like a connoiseur. He had been in the habit of rowing in his younger days, he said, and when he had spat in his hands—and he went through the action of pulling the oars—he did not care a fig for anybody. He had beaten more than one Englishman formerly at the Joinville regattas. He grew quite excited at last and offered to make a bet that in a boat like that he could row six leagues an hour without exerting himself.

"Luncheon is ready," the waitress said, appearing at the entrance to the boathouse, and they all hurried off. But two young men had taken the very seats that Madame Dufour had selected and were eating their luncheon. No doubt they were the owners of the sculls, for they were in boating costume. They were stretched out, almost lying on the chairs; they were sun-browned and their thin cotton jerseys, with short sleeves, showed their bare arms, which were as strong as a blacksmith's. They were two strong, athletic fellows, who showed in all their movements that elasticity and grace of limb which can only be acquired by exercise and which is so different to the deformity with which monotonous heavy work stamps the mechanic.

They exchanged a rapid smile when they saw the mother and then a glance on seeing the daughter.

"Let us give up our place," one of them said; "it will make us acquainted with them."

The other got up immediately, and holding his black and red boating cap in his hand, he politely offered the ladies the only shady place in the garden. With many excuses they accepted, and that it might be more rural, they sat on the grass, without either tables or chairs.

The two young men took their plates, knives, forks, etc., to a table a little way off and began to eat again, and their bare arms, which they showed continually, rather embarrassed the girl. She even pretended to turn her head aside and not to see them, while Madame Dufour, who was rather bolder, tempted by feminine curiosity, looked at them every moment, and, no doubt, compared them with the secret unsightliness of her husband. She had squatted herself on ground, with her legs tucked under her, after the manner of tailors, and she kept moving about restlessly, saying that ants were crawling about her somewhere. Monsieur Dufour, annoyed at the presence of the polite strangers, was trying to find a comfortable position which he did not, however, succeed in doing, and the young man with the yellow hair was eating as silently as an ogre.

"It is lovely weather, monsieur," the stout lady said to one of the boating men. She wished to be friendly because they had given up their place.

"It is, indeed, madame," he replied. "Do you often go into the country?"

"Oh, only once or twice a year to get a little fresh air. And you, monsieur?"

"I come and sleep here every night."

"Oh, that must be very nice!"

"Certainly it is, madame." And he gave them such a practical account of his daily life that it awakened afresh in the hearts of these shopkeepers who were deprived of the meadows and who longed for country walks, to that foolish love of nature which they all feel so strongly the whole year round behind the counter in their shop.

The girl raised her eyes and looked at the oarsman with emotion and Monsieur Dufour spoke for the first time.

"It is indeed a happy life," he said. And then he added: "A little more rabbit, my dear?"

"No, thank you," she replied, and turning to the young men again, and pointing to their arms, asked: "Do you never feel cold like that?"

They both began to laugh, and they astonished the family with an account of the enormous fatigue they could endure, of their bathing while in a state of tremendous perspiration, of their rowing in the fog at night; and they struck their chests violently to show how hollow they sounded.

"Ah! You look very strong," said the husband, who did not talk any more of the time when he used to beat the English. The girl was looking at them sideways now, and the young fellow with the yellow hair, who had swallowed some wine the wrong way, was coughing violently and bespattering Madame Dufour's cherry-colored silk dress. She got angry and sent for some water to wash the spots.

Meanwhile it had grown unbearably hot, the sparkling river looked like a blaze of fire and the fumes of the wine were getting into their heads. Monsieur Dufour, who had a violent hiccough, had unbuttoned his waistcoat and the top button of his trousers, while his wife, who felt choking, was gradually unfastening her dress. The apprentice was shaking his yellow wig in a happy frame of mind, and kept helping himself to wine, and the old grandmother, feeling the effects of the wine, was very stiff and dignified. As for the girl, one noticed only a peculiar brightness in her eyes, while the brown cheeks became more rosy.

The coffee finished, they suggested singing, and each of them sang or repeated a couplet, which the others applauded frantically. Then they got up with some difficulty, and while the two women, who were rather dizzy, were trying to get a breath of air, the two men, who were altogether drunk, were attempting gymnastics. Heavy, limp and with scarlet faces they hung or, awkwardly to the iron rings, without being able to raise themselves.

Meanwhile the two boating men had got their boats into the water, and they came back and politely asked the ladies whether they would like a row.

"Would you like one, Monsieur Dufour?" his wife exclaimed. "Please come!"

He merely gave her a drunken nod, without understanding what she said. Then one of the rowers came up with two fishing rods in his hands, and the hope of catching a gudgeon, that great vision of the Parisian shopkeeper, made Dufour's dull eyes gleam, and he politely allowed them to do whatever they liked, while he sat in the shade under the bridge, with his feet dangling over the river, by the side of the young man with the yellow hair, who was sleeping soundly.

One of the boating men made a martyr of himself and took the mother.

"Let us go to the little wood on the Ile aux Anglais!" he called out as he rowed off. The other boat went more slowly, for the rower was looking at his companion so intently that by thought of nothing else, and his emotion seemed to paralyze his strength, while the girl, who was sitting in the bow, gave herself up to the enjoyment of being on the water. She felt a disinclination to think, a lassitude in her limbs and a total enervation, as if she were intoxicated, and her face was flushed and her breathing quickened. The effects of the wine, which were increased by the extreme heat, made all the trees on the bank seem to bow as she passed. A vague wish for enjoyment and a fermentation of her blood seemed to pervade her whole body, which was excited by the heat of the day, and she was also disturbed at this tete-a-tete on the water, in a place which seemed depopulated by the heat, with this young man who thought her pretty, whose ardent looks seemed to caress her skin and were as penetrating and pervading as the sun's rays.

Their inability to speak increased their emotion, and they looked about them. At last, however, he made an effort and asked her name.

"Henriette," she said.

"Why, my name is Henri," he replied. The sound of their voices had calmed them, and they looked at the banks. The other boat had passed them and seemed to be waiting for them, and the rower called out:

"We will meet you in the wood; we are going as far as Robinson's, because Madame Dufour is thirsty." Then he bent over his oars again and rowed off so quickly that he was soon out of sight.

Meanwhile a continual roar, which they had heard for some time, came nearer, and the river itself seemed to shiver, as if the dull noise were rising from its depths.

"What is that noise?" she asked. It was the noise of the weir which cut the river in two at the island, and he was explaining it to her, when, above the noise of the waterfall, they heard the song of a bird, which seemed a long way off.

"Listen!" he said; "the nightingales are singing during the day, so the female birds must be sitting."

A nightingale! She had never heard one before, and the idea of listening to one roused visions of poetic tenderness in her heart. A nightingale! That is to say, the invisible witness of her love trysts which Juliet invoked on her balcony; that celestial music which it attuned to human kisses, that eternal inspirer of all those languorous romances which open an ideal sky to all the poor little tender hearts of sensitive girls!

She was going to hear a nightingale.

"We must not make a noise," her companion said, "and then we can go into the wood, and sit down close beside it."

The boat seemed to glide. They saw the trees on the island, the banks of which were so low that they could look into the depths of the thickets. They stopped, he made the boat fast, Henriette took hold of Henri's arm, and they went beneath the trees.

"Stoop," he said, so she stooped down, and they went into an inextricable thicket of creepers, leaves and reed grass, which formed an undiscoverable retreat, and which the young man laughingly called "his private room."

Just above their heads, perched in one of the trees which hid them, the bird was still singing. He uttered trills and roulades, and then loud, vibrating notes that filled the air and seemed to lose themselves on the horizon, across the level country, through that burning silence which weighed upon the whole landscape. They did not speak for fear of frightening it away. They were sitting close together, and, slowly, Henri's arm stole round the girl's waist and squeezed it gently. She took that daring hand without any anger, and kept removing it whenever he put it round her; without, however, feeling at all embarrassed by this caress, just as if it had been something quite natural, which she was resisting just as naturally.

She was listening to the bird in ecstasy. She felt an infinite longing for happiness, for some sudden demonstration of tenderness, for the revelation of superhuman poetry, and she felt such a softening at her heart, and relaxation of her nerves, that she began to cry, without knowing why. The young man was now straining her close to him, yet she did not remove his arm; she did not think of it. Suddenly the nightingale stopped, and a voice called out in the distance:

"Henriette!"

"Do not reply," he said in a low voice; "you will drive the bird away."

But she had no idea of doing so, and they remained in the same position for some time. Madame Dufour had sat down somewhere or other, for from time to time they heard the stout lady break out into little bursts of laughter.

The girl was still crying; she was filled with strange sensations. Henri's head was on her shoulder, and suddenly he kissed her on the lips. She was surprised and angry, and, to avoid him, she stood up.

They were both very pale when they left their grassy retreat. The blue sky appeared to them clouded and the ardent sun darkened; and they felt the solitude and the silence. They walked rapidly, side by side, without speaking or touching each other, for they seemed to have become irreconcilable enemies, as if disgust and hatred had arisen between them, and from time to time Henriette called out: "Mamma!"

By and by they heard a noise behind a bush, and the stout lady appeared, looking rather confused, and her companion's face was wrinkled with smiles which he could not check.

Madame Dufour took his arm, and they returned to the boats, and Henri, who was ahead, walked in silence beside the young girl. At last they got back to Bezons. Monsieur Dufour, who was now sober, was waiting for them very impatiently, while the young man with the yellow hair was having a mouthful of something to eat before leaving the inn. The carriage was waiting in the yard, and the grandmother, who had already got in, was very frightened at the thought of being overtaken by night before they reached Paris, as the outskirts were not safe.

They all shook bands, and the Dufour family drove off.

"Good-by, until we meet again!" the oarsmen cried, and the answer they got was a sigh and a tear.

Two months later, as Henri was going along the Rue des Martyrs, he saw Dufour, Ironmonger, over a door, and so he went in, and saw the stout lady sitting at the counter. They recognized each other immediately, and after an interchange of polite greetings, he asked after them all.

"And how is Mademoiselle Henriette?" he inquired specially.

"Very well, thank you; she is married."

"Ah!" He felt a certain emotion, but said: "Whom did she marry?"

"That young man who accompanied us, you know; he has joined us in business."

"I remember him perfectly."

He was going out, feeling very unhappy, though scarcely knowing why, when madame called him back.

"And how is your friend?" she asked rather shyly.

"He is very well, thank you."

"Please give him our compliments, and beg him to come and call, when he is in the neighborhood."

She then added: "Tell him it will give me great pleasure."

"I will be sure to do so. Adieu!"

"Do not say that; come again very soon."

The next year, one very hot Sunday, all the details of that adventure, which Henri had never forgotten, suddenly came back to him so clearly that he returned alone to their room in the wood, and was overwhelmed with astonishment when he went in. She was sitting on the grass, looking very sad, while by her side, still in his shirt sleeves, the young man with the yellow hair was sleeping soundly, like some animal.

She grew so pale when she saw Henri that at first he thought she was going to faint; then, however, they began to talk quite naturally. But when he told her that he was very fond of that spot, and went there frequently on Sundays to indulge in memories, she looked into his eyes for a long time.

"I too, think of it," she replied.

"Come, my dear," her husband said, with a yawn. "I think it is time for us to be going."

ROSE

The two young women appear to be buried under a blanket of flowers. They are alone in the immense landau, which is filled with flowers like a giant basket. On the front seat are two small hampers of white satin filled with violets, and on the bearskin by which their knees are covered there is a mass of roses, mimosas, pinks, daisies, tuberoses and orange blossoms, interwoven with silk ribbons; the two frail bodies seem buried under this beautiful perfumed bed, which hides everything but the shoulders and arms and a little of the dainty waists.

The coachman's whip is wound with a garland of anemones, the horses' traces are dotted with carnations, the spokes of the wheels are clothed in mignonette, and where the lanterns ought to be are two enormous round bouquets which look as though they were the eyes of this strange, rolling, flower-bedecked creature.

The landau drives rapidly along the road, through the Rue d'Antibes, preceded, followed, accompanied, by a crowd of other carriages covered with flowers, full of women almost hidden by a sea of violets. It is the flower carnival at Cannes.

The carriage reaches the Boulevard de la Fonciere, where the battle is waged. All along the immense avenue a double row of flower-bedecked vehicles are going and coming like an endless ribbon. Flowers are thrown from one to the other. They pass through the air like balls, striking fresh faces, bouncing and falling into the dust, where an army of youngsters pick them up.

A thick crowd is standing on the sidewalks looking on and held in check by the mounted police, who pass brutally along pushing back the curious pedestrians as though to prevent the common people from mingling with the rich.

In the carriages, people call to each other, recognize each other and bombard each other with roses. A chariot full of pretty women, dressed in red, like devils, attracts the eyes of all. A gentleman, who looks like the portraits of Henry IV., is throwing an immense bouquet which is held back by an elastic. Fearing the shock, the women hide their eyes and the men lower their heads, but the graceful, rapid and obedient missile describes a curve and returns to its master, who immediately throws it at some new face.

The two young women begin to throw their stock of flowers by handfuls, and receive a perfect hail of bouquets; then, after an hour of warfare, a little tired, they tell the coachman to drive along the road which follows the seashore.

The sun disappears behind Esterel, outlining the dark, rugged mountain against the sunset sky. The clear blue sea, as calm as a mill-pond, stretches out as far as the horizon, where it blends with the sky; and the fleet, anchored in the middle of the bay, looks like a herd of enormous beasts, motionless on the water, apocalyptic animals, armored and hump-backed, their frail masts looking like feathers, and with eyes which light up when evening approaches.

The two young women, leaning back under the heavy robes, look out lazily over the blue expanse of water. At last one of them says:

"How delightful the evenings are! How good everything seems! Don't you think so, Margot?"

"Yes, it is good. But there is always something lacking."

"What is lacking? I feel perfectly happy. I don't need anything else."

"Yes, you do. You are not thinking of it. No matter how contented we may be, physically, we always long for something more—for the heart."

The other asked with a smile:

"A little love?"

"Yes."

They stopped talking, their eyes fastened on the distant horizon, then the one called Marguerite murmured: "Life without that seems to me unbearable. I need to be loved, if only by a dog. But we are all alike, no matter what you may say, Simone."

"Not at all, my dear. I had rather not be loved at all than to be loved by the first comer. Do you think, for instance, that it would be pleasant to be loved by—by—"

She was thinking by whom she might possibly be loved, glancing across the wide landscape. Her eyes, after traveling around the horizon, fell on the two bright buttons which were shining on the back of the coachman's livery, and she continued, laughing: "by my coachman?"

Madame Margot barely smiled, and said in a low tone of voice:

"I assure you that it is very amusing to be loved by a servant. It has happened to me two or three times. They roll their eyes in such a funny manner—it's enough to make you die laughing! Naturally, the more in love they are, the more severe one must be with them, and then, some day, for some reason, you dismiss them, because, if anyone should notice it, you would appear so ridiculous."

Madame Simone was listening, staring straight ahead of her, then she remarked:

"No, I'm afraid that my footman's heart would not satisfy me. Tell me how you noticed that they loved you."

"I noticed it the same way that I do with other men—when they get stupid."

"The others don't seem stupid to me, when they love me."

"They are idiots, my dear, unable to talk, to answer, to understand anything."

"But how did you feel when you were loved by a servant? Were you—moved—flattered?"

"Moved? no, flattered—yes a little. One is always flattered to be loved by a man, no matter who he may be."

"Oh, Margot!"

"Yes, indeed, my dear! For instance, I will tell you of a peculiar incident which happened to me. You will see how curious and complex our emotions are, in such cases.

"About four years ago I happened to be without a maid. I had tried five or six, one right after the other, and I was about ready to give up in despair, when I saw an advertisement in a newspaper of a young girl knowing how to cook, embroider, dress hair, who was looking for a position and who could furnish the best of references. Besides all these accomplishments, she could speak English.

"I wrote to the given address, and the next day the person in question presented herself. She was tall, slender, pale, shy-looking. She had beautiful black eyes and a charming complexion; she pleased me immediately. I asked for her certificates; she gave me one in English, for she came, as she said, from Lady Rymwell's, where she had been for ten years.

"The certificate showed that the young girl had left of her own free will, in order to return to France, and the only thing which they had had to find fault in her during her long period of service was a little French coquettishness.

"This prudish English phrase even made me smile, and I immediately engaged this maid.

"She came to me the same day. Her name was Rose.

"At the end of a month I would have been helpless without her. She was a treasure, a pearl, a phenomenon.

"She could dress my hair with infinite taste; she could trim a hat better than most milliners, and she could even make my dresses.

"I was astonished at her accomplishments. I had never before been waited on in such a manner.

"She dressed me rapidly and with a surprisingly light touch. I never felt her fingers on my skin, and nothing is so disagreeable to me as contact with a servant's hand. I soon became excessively lazy; it was so pleasant to be dressed from head to foot, and from lingerie to gloves, by this tall, timid girl, always blushing a little, and never saying a word. After my bath she would rub and massage me while I dozed a little on my couch; I almost considered her more of a friend than a servant.

"One morning the janitor asked, mysteriously, to speak to me. I was surprised, and told him to come in. He was a good, faithful man, an old soldier, one of my husband's former orderlies.

"He seemed to be embarrassed by what he had to say to me. At last he managed to mumble:

"'Madame, the superintendent of police is downstairs.'

"I asked quickly:

"'What does he wish?'

"'He wishes to search the house.'

"Of course the police are useful, but I hate them. I do not think that it is a noble profession. I answered, angered and hurt:

"'Why this search? For what reason? He shall not come in.'

"The janitor continued:

"'He says that there is a criminal hidden in the house.'

"This time I was frightened and I told him to bring the inspector to me, so that I might get some explanation. He was a man with good manners and decorated with the Legion of Honor. He begged my pardon for disturbing me, and then informed me that I had, among my domestics, a convict.

"I was shocked; and I answered that I could guarantee every servant in the house, and I began to enumerate them.

"'The janitor, Pierre Courtin, an old soldier.'

"'It's not he.'

"'A stable-boy, son of farmers whom I know, and a groom whom you have just seen.'

"'It's not he.'

"'Then, monsieur, you see that you must be mistaken.'

"'Excuse me, madame, but I am positive that I am not making a mistake.

"As the conviction of a notable criminal is at stake, would you be so kind as to send for all your servants?"

"At first I refused, but I finally gave in, and sent downstairs for everybody, men and women.

"The inspector glanced at them and then declared:

"'This isn't all.'

"'Excuse me, monsieur, there is no one left but my maid, a young girl whom you could not possibly mistake for a convict.'

"He asked:

"'May I also see her?'

"'Certainly.'

"I rang for Rose, who immediately appeared. She had hardly entered the room, when the inspector made a motion, and two men whom I had not seen, hidden behind the door, sprang forward, seized her and tied her hands behind her back.

"I cried out in anger and tried to rush forward to defend her. The inspector stopped me:

"'This girl, madame, is a man whose name is Jean Nicolas Lecapet, condemned to death in 1879 for assaulting a woman and injuring her so that death resulted. His sentence was commuted to imprisonment for life. He escaped four months ago. We have been looking for him ever since.'

"I was terrified, bewildered. I did not believe him. The commissioner continued, laughing:

"'I can prove it to you. His right arm is tattooed.'

"'The sleeve was rolled up. It was true. The inspector added, with bad taste:

"'You can trust us for the other proofs.'

"And they led my maid away!

"Well, would you believe me, the thing that moved me most was not anger at having thus been played upon, deceived and made ridiculous, it was not the shame of having thus been dressed and undressed, handled and touched by this man—but a deep humiliation—a woman's humiliation. Do you understand?"

"I am afraid I don't."

"Just think—this man had been condemned for—for assaulting a woman. Well! I thought of the one whom he had assaulted—and—and I felt humiliated—There! Do you understand now?"

Madame Margot did not answer. She was looking straight ahead, her eyes fastened on the two shining buttons of the livery, with that sphinx-like smile which women sometimes have.

ROSALIE PRUDENT

There was a real mystery in this affair which neither the jury, nor the president, nor the public prosecutor himself could understand.

The girl Prudent (Rosalie), servant at the Varambots', of Nantes, having become enceinte without the knowledge of her masters, had, during the night, killed and buried her child in the garden.

It was the usual story of the infanticides committed by servant girls. But there was one inexplicable circumstance about this one. When the police searched the girl Prudent's room they discovered a complete infant's outfit, made by Rosalie herself, who had spent her nights for the last three months in cutting and sewing it. The grocer from whom she had bought her candles, out of her own wages, for this long piece of work had come to testify. It came out, moreover, that the sage-femme of the district, informed by Rosalie of her condition, had given her all necessary instructions and counsel in case the event should happen at a time when it might not be possible to get help. She had also procured a place at Poissy for the girl Prudent, who foresaw that her present employers would discharge her, for the Varambot couple did not trifle with morality.

There were present at the trial both the man and the woman, a middle-class pair from the provinces, living on their income. They were so exasperated against this girl, who had sullied their house, that they would have liked to see her guillotined on the spot without a trial. The spiteful depositions they made against her became accusations in their mouths.

The defendant, a large, handsome girl of Lower Normandy, well educated for her station in life, wept continuously and would not answer to anything.

The court and the spectators were forced to the opinion that she had committed this barbarous act in a moment of despair and madness, since there was every indication that she had expected to keep and bring up her child.

The president tried for the last time to make her speak, to get some confession, and, having urged her with much gentleness, he finally made her understand that all these men gathered here to pass judgment upon her were not anxious for her death and might even have pity on her.

Then she made up her mind to speak.

"Come, now, tell us, first, who is the father of this child?" he asked.

Until then she had obstinately refused to give his name.

But she replied suddenly, looking at her masters who had so cruelly calumniated her:

"It is Monsieur Joseph, Monsieur Varambot's nephew."

The couple started in their seats and cried with one voice—"That's not true! She lies! This is infamous!"

The president had them silenced and continued, "Go on, please, and tell us how it all happened."

Then she suddenly began to talk freely, relieving her pent-up heart, that poor, solitary, crushed heart—laying bare her sorrow, her whole sorrow, before those severe men whom she had until now taken for enemies and inflexible judges.

"Yes, it was Monsieur Joseph Varambot, when he came on leave last year."

"What does Mr. Joseph Varambot do?"

"He is a non-commissioned officer in the artillery, monsieur. Well, he stayed two months at the house, two months of the summer. I thought nothing about it when he began to look at me, and then flatter me, and make love to me all day long. And I let myself be taken in, monsieur. He kept saying to me that I was a handsome girl, that I was good company, that I just suited him—and I, I liked him well enough. What could I do? One listens to these things

14

when one is alone—all alone—as I was. I am alone in the world, monsieur. I have no one to talk to—no one to tell my troubles to. I have no father, no mother, no brother, no sister, nobody. And when he began to talk to me it was as if I had a brother who had come back. And then he asked me to go with him to the river one evening, so that we might talk without disturbing any one. I went—I don't know—I don't know how it happened. He had his arm around me. Really I didn't want to—no—no—I could not—I felt like crying, the air was so soft—the moon was shining. No, I swear to you—I could not—he did what he wanted. That went on three weeks, as long as he stayed. I could have followed him to the ends of the world. He went away. I did not know that I was enceinte. I did not know it until the month after—"

She began to cry so bitterly that they had to give her time to collect herself.

Then the president resumed with the tone of a priest at the confessional: "Come, now, go on."

She began to talk again: "When I realized my condition I went to see Madame Boudin, who is there to tell you, and I asked her how it would be, in case it should come if she were not there. Then I made the outfit, sewing night after night, every evening until one o'clock in the morning; and then I looked for another place, for I knew very well that I should be sent away, but I wanted to stay in the house until the very last, so as to save my pennies, for I have not got very much and I should need my money for the little one."

"Then you did not intend to kill him?"

"Oh, certainly not, monsieur!"

"Why did you kill him, then?"

"It happened this way. It came sooner than I expected. It came upon me in the kitchen, while I was doing the dishes. Monsieur and Madame Varambot were already asleep, so I went up, not without difficulty, dragging myself up by the banister, and I lay down on the bare floor. It lasted perhaps one hour, or two, or three; I don't know, I had such pain; and then I pushed him out with all my strength. I felt that he came out and I picked him up.

"Ah! but I was glad, I assure you! I did all that Madame Boudin told me to do. And then I laid him on my bed. And then such a pain griped me again that I thought I should die. If you knew what it meant, you there, you would not do so much of this. I fell on my knees, and then toppled over backward on the floor; and it griped me again, perhaps one hour, perhaps two. I lay there all alone—and then another one comes—another little one—two, yes, two, like this. I took him up as I did the first one, and then I put him on the bed, the two side by side. Is it possible, tell me, two children, and I who get only twenty francs a month? Say, is it possible? One, yes, that can be managed by going without things, but not two. That turned my head. What do I know about it? Had I any choice, tell me?

"What could I do? I felt as if my last hour had come. I put the pillow over them, without knowing why. I could not keep them both; and then I threw myself down, and I lay there, rolling over and over and crying until I saw the daylight come into the window. Both of them were quite dead under the pillow. Then I took them under my arms and went down the stairs out in the vegetable garden. I took the gardener's spade and I buried them under the earth, digging as deep a hole as I could, one here and the other one there, not together, so that they might not talk of their mother if these little dead bodies can talk. What do I know about it?

"And then, back in my bed, I felt so sick that I could not get up. They sent for the doctor and he understood it all. I'm telling you the truth, Your Honor. Do what you like with me; I'm ready."

Half of the jury were blowing their noses violently to keep from crying. The women in the courtroom were sobbing.

The president asked her:

"Where did you bury the other one?"

"The one that you have?" she asked.

"Why, this one—this one was in the artichokes."

"Oh, then the other one is among the strawberries, by the well."

And she began to sob so piteously that no one could hear her unmoved.

The girl Rosalie Prudent was acquitted.

REGRET

Monsieur Saval, who was called in Mantes "Father Saval," had just risen from bed. He was weeping. It was a dull autumn day; the leaves were falling. They fell slowly in the rain, like a heavier and slower rain. M. Saval was not in good spirits. He walked from the fireplace to the window, and from the window to the fireplace. Life has its sombre days. It would no longer have any but sombre days for him, for he had reached the age of sixty-two. He is alone, an old bachelor, with nobody about him. How sad it is to die alone, all alone, without any one who is devoted to you!

He pondered over his life, so barren, so empty. He recalled former days, the days of his childhood, the home, the house of his parents; his college days, his follies; the time he studied law in Paris, his father's illness, his death. He then returned to live with his mother. They lived together very quietly, and desired nothing more. At last the mother died. How sad life is! He lived alone since then, and now, in his turn, he, too, will soon be dead. He will disappear, and that will be the end. There will be no more of Paul Saval upon the earth. What a frightful thing! Other people will love, will laugh. Yes, people will go on amusing themselves, and he will no longer exist! Is it not strange that people can laugh, amuse themselves, be joyful under that eternal certainty of death? If this death were only probable, one could then have hope; but no, it is inevitable, as inevitable as that night follows the day.

If, however, his life had been full! If he had done something; if he had had adventures, great pleasures, success, satisfaction of some kind or another. But no, nothing. He had done nothing, nothing but rise from bed, eat, at the same hours, and go to bed again. And he had gone on like that to the age of sixty-two years. He had not even taken unto himself a wife, as other men do. Why? Yes, why was it that he had not married? He might have done so, for he possessed considerable means. Had he lacked an opportunity? Perhaps! But one can create opportunities. He was indifferent; that was all. Indifference had been his greatest drawback, his defect, his vice. How many men wreck their lives through indifference! It is so difficult for some natures to get out of bed, to move about, to take long walks, to speak, to study any question.

He had not even been loved. No woman had reposed on his bosom, in a complete abandon of love. He knew nothing of the delicious anguish of expectation, the divine vibration of a hand in yours, of the ecstasy of triumphant passion.

What superhuman happiness must overflow your heart, when lips encounter lips for the first time, when the grasp of four arms makes one being of you, a being unutterably happy, two beings infatuated with one another.

M. Saval was sitting before the fire, his feet on the fender, in his dressing gown. Assuredly his life had been spoiled, completely spoiled. He had, however, loved. He had loved secretly, sadly, and indifferently, in a manner characteristic of him in everything. Yes, he had loved his old friend, Madame Sandres, the wife of his old companion, Sandres. Ah! if he had known her as a young girl! But he had met her too late; she was already married. Unquestionably, he would have asked her hand! How he had loved her, nevertheless, without respite, since the first day he set eyes on her!

He recalled his emotion every time he saw her, his grief on leaving her, the many nights that he could not sleep, because he was thinking of her.

On rising in the morning he was somewhat more rational than on the previous evening. Why?

How pretty she was formerly, so dainty, with fair curly hair, and always laughing. Sandres was not the man she should have chosen. She was now fifty-two years of age. She seemed happy. Ah! if she had only loved him in days gone by; yes, if she had only loved him! And why should she not have loved him, he, Saval, seeing that he loved her so much, yes, she, Madame Sandres!

If only she could have guessed. Had she not guessed anything, seen anything, comprehended anything? What would she have thought? If he had spoken, what would she have answered?

And Saval asked himself a thousand other things. He reviewed his whole life, seeking to recall a multitude of details.

He recalled all the long evenings spent at the house of Sandres, when the latter's wife was young, and so charming.

He recalled many things that she had said to him, the intonations of her voice, the little significant smiles that meant so much.

He recalled their walks, the three of them together, along the banks of the Seine, their luncheon on the grass on Sundays, for Sandres was employed at the sub-prefecture. And all at once the distinct recollection came to him of an afternoon spent with her in a little wood on the banks of the river.

They had set out in the morning, carrying their provisions in baskets. It was a bright spring morning, one of those days which intoxicate one. Everything smells fresh, everything seems happy. The voices of the birds sound more joyous, and they fly more swiftly. They had luncheon on the grass, under the willow trees, quite close to the water, which glittered in the sun's rays. The air was balmy, charged with the odors of fresh vegetation; they drank it in with delight. How pleasant everything was on that day!

After lunch, Sandres went to sleep on the broad of his back. "The best nap he had in his life," said he, when he woke up.

Madame Sandres had taken the arm of Saval, and they started to walk along the river bank.

She leaned tenderly on his arm. She laughed and said to him: "I am intoxicated, my friend, I am quite intoxicated." He looked at her, his heart going pit-a-pat. He felt himself grow pale, fearful that he might have looked too boldly at her, and that the trembling of his hand had revealed his passion.

She had made a wreath of wild flowers and water-lilies, and she asked him: "Do I look pretty like that?"

As he did not answer—for he could find nothing to say, he would have liked to go down on his knees—she burst out laughing, a sort of annoyed, displeased laugh, as she said: "Great goose, what ails you? You might at least say something."

He felt like crying, but could not even yet find a word to say.

All these things came back to him now, as vividly as on the day when they took place. Why had she said this to him, "Great goose, what ails you? You might at least say something!"

And he recalled how tenderly she had leaned on his arm. And in passing under a shady tree he had felt her ear brushing his cheek, and he had moved his head abruptly, lest she should suppose he was too familiar.

When he had said to her: "Is it not time to return?" she darted a singular look at him. "Certainly," she said, "certainly," regarding him at the same time in a curious manner. He had not thought of it at the time, but now the whole thing appeared to him quite plain.

"Just as you like, my friend. If you are tired let us go back."

And he had answered: "I am not fatigued; but Sandres may be awake now."

And she had said: "If you are afraid of my husband's being awake, that is another thing. Let us return."

On their way back she remained silent, and leaned no longer on his arm. Why?

At that time it had never occurred to him, to ask himself "why." Now he seemed to apprehend something that he had not then understood.

Could it?

M. Saval felt himself blush, and he got up at a bound, as if he were thirty years younger and had heard Madame Sandres say, "I love you."

Was it possible? That idea which had just entered his mind tortured him. Was it possible that he had not seen, had not guessed?

Oh! if that were true, if he had let this opportunity of happiness pass without taking advantage of it!

He said to himself: "I must know. I cannot remain in this state of doubt. I must know!" He thought: "I am sixty-two years of age, she is fifty-eight; I may ask her that now without giving offense."

He started out.

The Sandres' house was situated on the other side of the street, almost directly opposite his own. He went across and knocked at the door, and a little servant opened it.

"You here at this hour, Saval! Has some accident happened to you?"

"No, my girl," he replied; "but go and tell your mistress that I want to speak to her at once."

"The fact is madame is preserving pears for the winter, and she is in the preserving room. She is not dressed, you understand."

"Yes, but go and tell her that I wish to see her on a very important matter."

The little servant went away, and Saval began to walk, with long, nervous strides, up and down the drawing-room. He did not feel in the least embarrassed, however. Oh! he was merely going to ask her something, as he would have asked her about some cooking recipe. He was sixty-two years of age!

The door opened and madame appeared. She was now a large woman, fat and round, with full cheeks and a sonorous laugh. She walked with her arms away from her sides and her sleeves tucked up, her bare arms all covered with fruit juice. She asked anxiously:

"What is the matter with you, my friend? You are not ill, are you?"

"No, my dear friend; but I wish to ask you one thing, which to me is of the first importance, something which is torturing my heart, and I want you to promise that you will answer me frankly."

She laughed, "I am always frank. Say on."

"Well, then. I have loved you from the first day I ever saw you. Can you have any doubt of this?"

She responded, laughing, with something of her former tone of voice.

"Great goose! what ails you? I knew it from the very first day!"

Saval began to tremble. He stammered out: "You knew it? Then..."

He stopped.

She asked:

"Then?"

He answered:

"Then—what did you think? What—what—what would you have answered?"

She broke into a peal of laughter. Some of the juice ran off the tips of her fingers on to the carpet.

"What?"

"I? Why, you did not ask me anything. It was not for me to declare myself!"

He then advanced a step toward her.

"Tell me—tell me.... You remember the day when Sandres went to sleep on the grass after lunch... when we had walked together as far as the bend of the river, below..."

He waited, expectantly. She had ceased to laugh, and looked at him, straight in the eyes.

"Yes, certainly, I remember it."

He answered, trembling all over:

"Well—that day—if I had been—if I had been—venturesome—what would you have done?"

She began to laugh as only a happy woman can laugh, who has nothing to regret, and responded frankly, in a clear voice tinged with irony:

"I would have yielded, my friend."

She then turned on her heels and went back to her jam-making.

Saval rushed into the street, cast down, as though he had met with some disaster. He walked with giant strides through the rain, straight on, until he reached the river bank, without thinking where he was going. He then turned to the right and followed the river. He walked a long time, as if urged on by some instinct. His clothes were running with water, his hat was out of shape, as soft as a rag, and dripping like a roof. He walked on, straight in front of him. At last, he came to the place where they had lunched on that day so long ago, the recollection of which tortured his heart. He sat down under the leafless trees, and wept.

A SISTER'S CONFESSION

Marguerite de Therelles was dying. Although she was only fifty-six years old she looked at least seventy-five. She gasped for breath, her face whiter than the sheets, and had spasms of violent shivering, with her face convulsed and her eyes haggard as though she saw a frightful vision.

Her elder sister, Suzanne, six years older than herself, was sobbing on her knees beside the bed. A small table close to the dying woman's couch bore, on a white cloth, two lighted candles, for the priest was expected at any moment to administer extreme unction and the last communion.

The apartment wore that melancholy aspect common to death chambers; a look of despairing farewell. Medicine bottles littered the furniture; linen lay in the corners into which it had been kicked or swept. The very chairs looked, in their disarray, as if they were terrified and had run in all directions. Death—terrible Death—was in the room, hidden, awaiting his prey.

This history of the two sisters was an affecting one. It was spoken of far and wide; it had drawn tears from many eyes.

Suzanne, the elder, had once been passionately loved by a young man, whose affection she returned. They were engaged to be married, and the wedding day was at hand, when Henry de Sampierre suddenly died.

The young girl's despair was terrible, and she took an oath never to marry. She faithfully kept her vow and adopted widow's weeds for the remainder of her life.

But one morning her sister, her little sister Marguerite, then only twelve years old, threw herself into Suzanne's arms, sobbing: "Sister, I don't want you to be unhappy. I don't want you to mourn all your life. I'll never leave you—never, never, never! I shall never marry, either. I'll stay with you always—always!"

Suzanne kissed her, touched by the child's devotion, though not putting any faith in her promise.

But the little one kept her word, and, despite her parents' remonstrances, despite her elder sister's prayers, never married. She was remarkably pretty and refused many offers. She never left her sister.

They spent their whole life together, without a single day's separation. They went everywhere together and were inseparable. But Marguerite was pensive, melancholy, sadder than her sister, as if her sublime sacrifice had undermined her spirits. She grew older more quickly; her hair was white at thirty; and she was often ill, apparently stricken with some unknown, wasting malady.

And now she would be the first to die.

She had not spoken for twenty-four hours, except to whisper at daybreak:

"Send at once for the priest."

And she had since remained lying on her back, convulsed with agony, her lips moving as if unable to utter the dreadful words that rose in her heart, her face expressive of a terror distressing to witness.

Suzanne, distracted with grief, her brow pressed against the bed, wept bitterly, repeating over and over again the words:

"Margot, my poor Margot, my little one!"

She had always called her "my little one," while Marguerite's name for the elder was invariably "sister."

A footstep sounded on the stairs. The door opened. An acolyte appeared, followed by the aged priest in his surplice. As soon as she saw him the dying woman sat up suddenly in bed, opened her lips, stammered a few words and began to scratch the bed-clothes, as if she would have made hole in them.

Father Simon approached, took her hand, kissed her on the forehead and said in a gentle voice:

"May God pardon your sins, my daughter. Be of good courage. Now is the moment to confess them—speak!"

Then Marguerite, shuddering from head to foot, so that the very bed shook with her nervous movements, gasped:

"Sit down, sister, and listen."

The priest stooped toward the prostrate Suzanne, raised her to her feet, placed her in a chair, and, taking a hand of each of the sisters, pronounced:

"Lord God! Send them strength! Shed Thy mercy upon them."

And Marguerite began to speak. The words issued from her lips one by one—hoarse, jerky, tremulous.

"Pardon, pardon, sister! pardon me! Oh, if only you knew how I have dreaded this moment all my life!"

Suzanne faltered through her tears:

"But what have I to pardon, little one? You have given me everything, sacrificed all to me. You are an angel."

But Marguerite interrupted her:

"Be silent, be silent! Let me speak! Don't stop me! It is terrible. Let me tell all, to the very end, without interruption. Listen. You remember—you remember—Henry—"

Suzanne trembled and looked at her sister. The younger one went on:

"In order to understand you must hear everything. I was twelve years old—only twelve—you remember, don't you? And I was spoilt; I did just as I pleased. You remember how everybody spoilt me? Listen. The first time he came he had on his riding boots; he dismounted, saying that he had a message for father. You remember, don't you? Don't speak. Listen. When I saw him I was struck with admiration. I thought him so handsome, and I stayed in a corner of the drawing-room all the time he was talking. Children are strange—and terrible. Yes, indeed, I dreamt of him.

"He came again—many times. I looked at him with all my eyes, all my heart. I was large for my age and much more precocious than—any one suspected. He came often. I thought only of him. I often whispered to myself:

"'Henry-Henry de Sampierre!'

"Then I was told that he was going to marry you. That was a blow! Oh, sister, a terrible blow—terrible! I wept all through three sleepless nights.

"He came every afternoon after lunch. You remember, don't you? Don't answer. Listen. You used to make cakes that he was very fond of—with flour, butter and milk. Oh, I know how to make them. I could make them still, if necessary. He would swallow them at one mouthful and wash them down with a glass of wine, saying: 'Delicious!' Do you remember the way he said it?

"I was jealous—jealous! Your wedding day was drawing near. It was only a fortnight distant. I was distracted. I said to myself: 'He shall not marry Suzanne—no, he shall not! He shall marry me when I am old enough! I shall never love any one half so much.' But one evening, ten days before the wedding, you went for a stroll with him in the moonlight before the house—and yonder—under the pine tree, the big pine tree—he kissed you—kissed you—and held you in his arms so long—so long! You remember, don't you? It was probably the first time. You were so pale when you came back to the drawing-room!

"I saw you. I was there in the shrubbery. I was mad with rage! I would have killed you both if I could!

"I said to myself: 'He shall never marry Suzanne—never! He shall marry no one! I could not bear it.' And all at once I began to hate him intensely.

"Then do you know what I did? Listen. I had seen the gardener prepare pellets for killing stray dogs. He would crush a bottle into small pieces with a stone and put the ground glass into a ball of meat.

"I stole a small medicine bottle from mother's room. I ground it fine with a hammer and hid the glass in my pocket. It was a glistening powder. The next day, when you had made your little cakes; I opened them with a knife and inserted the glass. He ate three. I ate one myself. I threw the six others into the pond. The two swans died three days later. You remember? Oh, don't speak! Listen, listen. I, I alone did not die. But I have always been ill. Listen—he died—you know—listen—that was not the worst. It was afterward, later—always—the most terrible—listen.

"My life, all my life—such torture! I said to myself: 'I will never leave my sister. And on my deathbed I will tell her all.' And now I have told. And I have always thought of this moment—the moment when all would be told. Now it has come. It is terrible—oh!—sister—

"I have always thought, morning and evening, day and night: 'I shall have to tell her some day!' I waited. The horror of it! It is done. Say nothing. Now I am afraid—I am afraid! Oh! Supposing I should see him again, by and by, when I am dead! See him again! Only to think of it! I dare not—yet I must. I am going to die. I want you to forgive me. I insist on it. I cannot meet him without your forgiveness. Oh, tell her to forgive me, Father! Tell her. I implore you! I cannot die without it."

She was silent and lay back, gasping for breath, still plucking at the sheets with her fingers.

Suzanne had hidden her face in her hands and did not move. She was thinking of him whom she had loved so long. What a life of happiness they might have had together! She saw him again in the dim and distant past-that past forever lost. Beloved dead! how the thought of them rends the heart! Oh! that kiss, his only kiss! She had retained the memory of it in her soul. And, after that, nothing, nothing more throughout her whole existence!

The priest rose suddenly and in a firm, compelling voice said:

"Mademoiselle Suzanne, your sister is dying!"

Then Suzanne, raising her tear-stained face, put her arms round her sister, and kissing her fervently, exclaimed:

"I forgive you, I forgive you, little one!"

COCO

Throughout the whole countryside the Lucas farm, was known as "the Manor." No one knew why. The peasants doubtless attached to this word, "Manor," a meaning of wealth and of splendor, for this farm was undoubtedly the largest, richest and the best managed in the whole neighborhood.

The immense court, surrounded by five rows of magnificent trees, which sheltered the delicate apple trees from the harsh wind of the plain, inclosed in its confines long brick buildings used for storing fodder and grain, beautiful stables built of hard stone and made to accommodate thirty horses, and a red brick residence which looked like a little chateau.

Thanks for the good care taken, the manure heaps were as little offensive as such things can be; the watch-dogs lived in kennels, and countless poultry paraded through the tall grass.

Every day, at noon, fifteen persons, masters, farmhands and the women folks, seated themselves around the long kitchen table where the soup was brought in steaming in a large, blue-flowered bowl.

The beasts-horses, cows, pigs and sheep-were fat, well fed and clean. Maitre Lucas, a tall man who was getting stout, would go round three times a day, overseeing everything and thinking of everything.

A very old white horse, which the mistress wished to keep until its natural death, because she had brought it up and had always used it, and also because it recalled many happy memories, was housed, through sheer kindness of heart, at the end of the stable.

A young scamp about fifteen years old, Isidore Duval by name, and called, for convenience, Zidore, took care of this pensioner, gave him his measure of oats and fodder in winter, and in summer was supposed to change his pasturing place four times a day, so that he might have plenty of fresh grass.

The animal, almost crippled, lifted with difficulty his legs, large at the knees and swollen above the hoofs. His coat, which was no longer curried, looked like white hair, and his long eyelashes gave to his eyes a sad expression.

When Zidore took the animal to pasture, he had to pull on the rope with all his might, because it walked so slowly; and the youth, bent over and out of breath, would swear at it, exasperated at having to care for this old nag.

The farmhands, noticing the young rascal's anger against Coco, were amused and would continually talk of the horse to Zidore, in order to exasperate him. His comrades would make sport with him. In the village he was called Coco-Zidore.

The boy would fume, feeling an unholy desire to revenge himself on the horse. He was a thin, long-legged, dirty child, with thick, coarse, bristly red hair. He seemed only half-witted, and stuttered as though ideas were unable to form in his thick, brute-like mind.

For a long time he had been unable to understand why Coco should be kept, indignant at seeing things wasted on this useless beast. Since the horse could no longer work, it seemed to him unjust that he should be fed; he revolted at the idea of wasting oats, oats which were so expensive, on this paralyzed old plug. And often, in spite of the orders of Maitre Lucas, he would economize on the nag's food, only giving him half measure. Hatred grew in his confused, childlike mind, the hatred of a stingy, mean, fierce, brutal and cowardly peasant.

When summer came he had to move the animal about in the pasture. It was some distance away. The rascal, angrier every morning, would start, with his dragging step, across the wheat fields. The men working in the fields would shout to him, jokingly:

"Hey, Zidore, remember me to Coco."

He would not answer; but on the way he would break off a switch, and, as soon as he had moved the old horse, he would let it begin grazing; then, treacherously sneaking up behind it, he would slash its legs. The animal would try to escape, to kick, to get away from the blows, and run around in a circle about its rope, as though it had been inclosed in a circus ring. And the boy would slash away furiously, running along behind, his teeth clenched in anger.

Then he would go away slowly, without turning round, while the horse watched him disappear, his ribs sticking out, panting as a result of his unusual exertions. Not until the blue blouse of the young peasant was out of sight would he lower his thin white head to the grass.

As the nights were now warm, Coco was allowed to sleep out of doors, in the field behind the little wood. Zidore alone went to see him. The boy threw stones at him to amuse himself. He would sit down on an embankment about ten feet away and would stay there about half an hour, from time to time throwing a sharp stone at the old horse, which remained standing tied before his enemy, watching him continually and not daring to eat before he was gone.

This one thought persisted in the mind of the young scamp: "Why feed this horse, which is no longer good for anything?" It seemed to him that this old nag was stealing the food of the others, the goods of man and God, that he was even robbing him, Zidore, who was working.

Then, little by little, each day, the boy began to shorten the length of rope which allowed the horse to graze.

The hungry animal was growing thinner, and starving. Too feeble to break his bonds, he would stretch his head out toward the tall, green, tempting grass, so near that he could smell, and yet so far that he could not touch it.

But one morning Zidore had an idea: it was, not to move Coco any more. He was tired of walking so far for that old skeleton. He came, however, in order to enjoy his vengeance. The beast watched him anxiously. He did not beat him that day. He walked around him with his hands in his pockets. He even pretended to change his place, but he sank the stake in exactly the same hole, and went away overjoyed with his invention.

The horse, seeing him leave, neighed to call him back; but the rascal began to run, leaving him alone, entirely alone in his field, well tied down and without a blade of grass within reach.

Starving, he tried to reach the grass which he could touch with the end of his nose. He got on his knees, stretching out his neck and his long, drooling lips. All in vain. The old animal spent the whole day in useless, terrible efforts. The sight of all that green food, which stretched out on all sides of him, served to increase the gnawing pangs of hunger.

The scamp did not return that day. He wandered through the woods in search of nests.

The next day he appeared upon the scene again. Coco, exhausted, had lain down. When he saw the boy, he got up, expecting at last to have his place changed.

But the little peasant did not even touch the mallet, which was lying on the ground. He came nearer, looked at the animal, threw at his head a clump of earth which flattened out against the white hair, and he started off again, whistling.

The horse remained standing as long as he could see him; then, knowing that his attempts to reach the near-by grass would be hopeless, he once more lay down on his side and closed his eyes.

The following day Zidore did not come.

When he did come at last, he found Coco still stretched out; he saw that he was dead.

Then he remained standing, looking at him, pleased with what he had done, surprised that it should already be all over. He touched him with his foot, lifted one of his legs and then let it drop, sat on him and remained there, his eyes fixed on the grass, thinking of nothing. He returned to the farm, but did not mention the accident, because he wished to wander about at the hours when he used to change the horse's pasture. He went to see him the next day. At his approach some crows flew away. Countless flies were walking over the body and were buzzing around it. When he returned home, he announced the event. The animal was so old that nobody was surprised. The master said to two of the men:

"Take your shovels and dig a hole right where he is."

The men buried the horse at the place where he had died of hunger. And the grass grew thick, green and vigorous, fed by the poor body.

DEAD WOMAN'S SECRET

The woman had died without pain, quietly, as a woman should whose life had been blameless. Now she was resting in her bed, lying on her back, her eyes closed, her features calm, her long white hair carefully arranged as though she had done it up ten minutes before dying. The whole pale countenance of the dead woman was so collected, so calm, so resigned that one could feel what a sweet soul had lived in that body, what a quiet existence this old soul had led, how easy and pure the death of this parent had been.

Kneeling beside the bed, her son, a magistrate with inflexible principles, and her daughter, Marguerite, known as Sister Eulalie, were weeping as though their hearts would break. She had, from childhood up, armed them with a strict moral code, teaching them religion, without weakness, and duty, without compromise. He, the man, had become a judge and handled the law as a weapon with which he smote the weak ones without pity. She, the girl, influenced by the virtue which had bathed her in this austere family, had become the bride of the Church through her loathing for man.

They had hardly known their father, knowing only that he had made their mother most unhappy, without being told any other details.

The nun was wildly-kissing the dead woman's hand, an ivory hand as white as the large crucifix lying across the bed. On the other side of the long body the other hand seemed still to be holding the sheet in the death grasp; and the sheet had preserved the little creases as a memory of those last movements which precede eternal immobility.

A few light taps on the door caused the two sobbing heads to look up, and the priest, who had just come from dinner, returned. He was red and out of breath from his interrupted digestion, for he had made himself a strong mixture of coffee and brandy in order to combat the fatigue of the last few nights and of the wake which was beginning.

He looked sad, with that assumed sadness of the priest for whom death is a bread winner. He crossed himself and approaching with his professional gesture: "Well, my poor children! I have come to help you pass these last sad hours." But Sister Eulalie suddenly arose. "Thank you, father, but my brother and I prefer to remain alone with her. This is our last chance to see her, and we wish to be together, all three of us, as we—we—used to be when we were small and our poor mo—mother——"

Grief and tears stopped her; she could not continue.

Once more serene, the priest bowed, thinking of his bed. "As you wish, my children." He knelt, crossed himself, prayed, arose and went out quietly, murmuring: "She was a saint!"

They remained alone, the dead woman and her children. The ticking of the clock, hidden in the shadow, could be heard distinctly, and through the open window drifted in the sweet smell of hay and of woods, together with the soft moonlight. No other noise could be heard over the land except the occasional croaking of the frog or the chirping of some belated insect. An infinite peace, a divine melancholy, a silent serenity surrounded this dead woman, seemed to be breathed out from her and to appease nature itself.

Then the judge, still kneeling, his head buried in the bed clothes, cried in a voice altered by grief and deadened by the sheets and blankets: "Mamma, mamma, mamma!" And his sister, frantically striking her forehead against the woodwork, convulsed, twitching and trembling as in an epileptic fit, moaned: "Jesus, Jesus, mamma, Jesus!" And both of them, shaken by a storm of grief, gasped and choked.

The crisis slowly calmed down and they began to weep quietly, just as on the sea when a calm follows a squall.

A rather long time passed and they arose and looked at their dead. And the memories, those distant memories, yesterday so dear, to-day so torturing, came to their minds with all the little forgotten details, those little intimate familiar details which bring back to life the one who has left. They recalled to each other circumstances, words, smiles, intonations of the mother who was no longer to speak to them. They saw her again happy and calm. They remembered things which she had said, and a little motion of the hand, like beating time, which she often used when emphasizing something important.

And they loved her as they never had loved her before. They measured the depth of their grief, and thus they discovered how lonely they would find themselves.

It was their prop, their guide, their whole youth, all the best part of their lives which was disappearing. It was their bond with life, their mother, their mamma, the connecting link with their forefathers which they would thenceforth miss. They now became solitary, lonely beings; they could no longer look back.

The nun said to her brother: "You remember how mamma used always to read her old letters; they are all there in that drawer. Let us, in turn, read them; let us live her whole life through tonight beside her! It would be like a road to the cross, like making the acquaintance of her mother, of our grandparents, whom we never knew, but whose letters are there and of whom she so often spoke, do you remember?"

Out of the drawer they took about ten little packages of yellow paper, tied with care and arranged one beside the other. They threw these relics on the bed and chose one of them on which the word "Father" was written. They opened and read it.

It was one of those old-fashioned letters which one finds in old family desk drawers, those epistles which smell of another century. The first one started: "My dear," another one: "My beautiful little girl," others: "My dear child," or: "My dear (laughter)." And suddenly the nun began to read aloud, to read over to the dead woman her whole history, all her tender memories. The judge, resting his elbow on the bed, was listening with his eyes fastened on his mother. The motionless body seemed happy.

Sister Eulalie, interrupting herself, said suddenly:

"These ought to be put in the grave with her; they ought to be used as a shroud and she ought to be buried in it." She took another package, on which no name was written. She began to read in a firm voice: "My adored one, I love you wildly. Since yesterday I have been suffering the tortures of the damned, haunted by our memory. I feel your lips against mine, your eyes in mine, your breast against mine. I love you, I love you! You have driven me mad. My arms open, I gasp, moved by a wild desire to hold you again. My whole soul and body cries out for you, wants you. I have kept in my mouth the taste of your kisses—"

The judge had straightened himself up. The nun stopped reading. He snatched the letter from her and looked for the signature. There was none, but only under the words, "The man who adores you," the name "Henry." Their father's name was Rene. Therefore this was not from him. The son then quickly rummaged through the package of letters, took one out and read: "I can no longer live without your caresses." Standing erect, severe as when sitting on the bench, he looked unmoved at the dead woman. The nun, straight as a statue, tears trembling in the corners of her eyes, was watching her brother, waiting. Then he crossed the room slowly, went to the window and stood there, gazing out into the dark night.

When he turned around again Sister Eulalie, her eyes dry now, was still standing near the bed, her head bent down.

He stepped forward, quickly picked up the letters and threw them pell-mell back into the drawer. Then he closed the curtains of the bed.

When daylight made the candles on the table turn pale the son slowly left his armchair, and without looking again at the mother upon whom he had passed sentence, severing the tie that united her to son and daughter, he said slowly: "Let us now retire, sister."

A HUMBLE DRAMA

Meetings that are unexpected constitute the charm of traveling. Who has not experienced the joy of suddenly coming across a Parisian, a college friend, or a neighbor, five hundred miles from home? Who has not passed a night awake in one of those small, rattling country stage-coaches, in regions where steam is still a thing unknown, beside a strange young woman, of whom one has caught only a glimpse in the dim light of the lantern, as she entered the carriage in front of a white house in some small country town?

And the next morning, when one's head and ears feel numb with the continuous tinkling of the bells and the loud rattling of the windows, what a charming sensation it is to see your pretty neighbor open her eyes, startled, glance around her, arrange her rebellious hair with her slender fingers, adjust her hat, feel with sure hand whether her corset is still in place, her waist straight, and her skirt not too wrinkled.

She glances at you coldly and curiously. Then she leans back and no longer seems interested in anything but the country.

In spite of yourself, you watch her; and in spite of yourself you keep on thinking of her. Who is she? Whence does she come? Where is she going? In spite of yourself you spin a little romance around her. She is pretty; she seems charming! Happy he who... Life might be delightful with her. Who knows? She is perhaps the woman of our dreams, the one suited to our disposition, the one for whom our heart calls.

And how delicious even the disappointment at seeing her get out at the gate of a country house! A man stands there, who is awaiting her, with two children and two maids. He takes her in his arms and kisses as he lifts her out. Then she stoops over the little ones, who hold up their hands to her; she kisses them tenderly; and then they all go away together, down a path, while the maids catch the packages which the driver throws down to them from the coach.

Adieu! It is all over. You never will see her again! Adieu to the young woman who has passed the night by your side. You know her no more, you have not spoken to her; all the same, you feel a little sad to see her go. Adieu!

I have had many of these souvenirs of travel, some joyous and some sad.

Once I was in Auvergne, tramping through those delightful French mountains, that are not too high, not too steep, but friendly and familiar. I had climbed the Sancy, and entered a little inn, near a pilgrim's chapel called Notre-Dame de Vassiviere, when I saw a queer, ridiculous-looking old woman breakfasting alone at the end table.

She was at least seventy years old, tall, skinny, and angular, and her white hair was puffed around her temples in the old-fashioned style. She was dressed like a traveling Englishwoman, in awkward, queer clothing, like a person who is indifferent to dress. She was eating an omelet and drinking water.

Her face was peculiar, with restless eyes and the expression of one with whom fate has dealt unkindly. I watched her, in spite of myself, thinking: "Who is she? What is the life of this woman? Why is she wandering alone through these mountains?"

She paid and rose to leave, drawing up over her shoulders an astonishing little shawl, the two ends of which hung over her arms. From a corner of the room she took an alpenstock, which was covered with names traced with a hot iron; then she went out, straight, erect, with the long steps of a letter-carrier who is setting out on his route.

A guide was waiting for her at the door, and both went away. I watched them go down the valley, along the road marked by a line of high wooden crosses. She was taller than her companion, and seemed to walk faster than he.

Two hours later I was climbing the edge of the deep funnel that incloses Lake Pavin in a marvelous and enormous basin of verdure, full of trees, bushes, rocks, and flowers. This lake is so round that it seems as if the outline had been drawn with a pair of compasses, so clear and blue that one might deem it a flood of azure come down from the sky, so charming that one would like to live in a hut on the wooded slope which dominates this crater, where the cold, still water is sleeping. The Englishwoman was standing there like a statue, gazing upon the transparent sheet down in the dead volcano. She was straining her eyes to penetrate below the surface down to the unknown depths, where monstrous trout which have devoured all the other fish are said to live. As I was passing close by her, it seemed to me that two big tears were brimming her eyes. But she departed at a great pace, to rejoin her guide, who had stayed behind in an inn at the foot of the path leading to the lake.

I did not see her again that day.

The next day, at nightfall, I came to the chateau of Murol. The old fortress, an enormous tower standing on a peak in the midst of a large valley, where three valleys intersect, rears its brown, uneven, cracked surface into the sky; it is round, from its large circular base to the crumbling turrets on its pinnacles.

It astonishes the eye more than any other ruin by its simple mass, its majesty, its grave and imposing air of antiquity. It stands there, alone, high as a mountain, a dead queen, but still the queen of the valleys stretched out beneath it. You go up by a slope planted with firs, then you enter a narrow gate, and stop at the foot of the walls, in the first inclosure, in full view of the entire country.

Inside there are ruined halls, crumbling stairways, unknown cavities, dungeons, walls cut through in the middle, vaulted roofs held up one knows not how, and a mass of stones and crevices, overgrown with grass, where animals glide in and out.

I was exploring this ruin alone.

Suddenly I perceived behind a bit of wall a being, a kind of phantom, like the spirit of this ancient and crumbling habitation.

I was taken aback with surprise, almost with fear, when I recognized the old lady whom I had seen twice.

She was weeping, with big tears in her eyes, and held her handkerchief in her hand.

I turned around to go away, when she spoke to me, apparently ashamed to have been surprised in her grief.

"Yes, monsieur, I am crying. That does not happen often to me."

"Pardon me, madame, for having disturbed you," I stammered, confused, not knowing what to say. "Some misfortune has doubtless come to you."

"Yes. No—I am like a lost dog," she murmured, and began to sob, with her handkerchief over her eyes.

Moved by these contagious tears, I took her hand, trying to calm her. Then brusquely she told me her history, as if no longer ably to bear her grief alone.

"Oh! Oh! Monsieur—if you knew—the sorrow in which I live—in what sorrow.

"Once I was happy. I have a house down there—a home. I cannot go back to it any more; I shall never go back to it again, it is too hard to bear.

"I have a son. It is he! it is he! Children don't know. Oh, one has such a short time to live! If I should see him now I should perhaps not recognize him. How I loved him? How I loved him! Even before he was born, when I felt him move. And after that! How I have kissed and caressed and cherished him! If you knew how many nights I have passed in watching him sleep, and how many in thinking of him. I was crazy about him. When he was eight years old his father sent him to boarding-school. That was the end. He no longer belonged to me. Oh, heavens! He came to see me every Sunday. That was all!

"He went to college in Paris. Then he came only four times a year, and every time I was astonished to see how he had changed, to find him taller without having seen him grow. They stole his childhood from me, his confidence, and his love which otherwise would not have gone away from me; they stole my joy in seeing him grow, in seeing him become a little man.

"I saw him four times a year. Think of it! And at every one of his visits his body, his eye, his movements, his voice his laugh, were no longer the same, were no longer mine. All these things change so quickly in a child; and it is so sad if one is not there to see them change; one no longer recognizes him.

"One year he came with down on his cheek! He! my son! I was dumfounded —would you believe it? I hardly dared to kiss him. Was it really he, my little, little curly head of old, my dear; dear child, whom I had held in his diapers or my knee, and who had nursed at my breast with his little greedy lips—was it he, this tall, brown boy, who no longer knew how to kiss me, who seemed to love me as a matter of duty, who called me 'mother' for the sake of politeness, and who kissed me on the forehead, when I felt like crushing him in my arms?

"My husband died. Then my parents, and then my two sisters. When Death enters a house it seems as if he were hurrying to do his utmost, so as not to have to return for a long time after that. He spares only one or two to mourn the others.

"I remained alone. My tall son was then studying law. I was hoping to live and die near him, and I went to him so that we could live together. But he had fallen into the ways of young men, and he gave me to understand that I was in his way. So I left. I was wrong in doing so, but I suffered too much in feeling myself in his way, I, his mother! And I came back home.

"I hardly ever saw him again.

"He married. What a joy! At last we should be together for good. I should have grandchildren. His wife was an Englishwoman, who took a dislike to me. Why? Perhaps she thought that I loved him too much.

"Again I was obliged to go away. And I was alone. Yes, monsieur.

"Then he went to England, to live with them, with his wife's parents. Do you understand? They have him—they have my son for themselves. They have stolen him from me. He writes to me once a month. At first he came to see me. But now he no longer comes.

"It is now four years since I saw him last. His face then was wrinkled and his hair white. Was that possible? This man, my son, almost an old man? My little rosy child of old? No doubt I shall never see him again.

"And so I travel about all the year. I go east and west, as you see, with no companion.

"I am like a lost dog. Adieu, monsieur! don't stay here with me for it hurts me to have told you all this."

I went down the hill, and on turning round to glance back, I saw the old woman standing on a broken wall, looking out upon the mountains, the long valley and Lake Chambon in the distance.

And her skirt and the queer little shawl which she wore around her thin shoulders were fluttering like a flag in the wind.

MADEMOISELLE COCOTTE

We were just leaving the asylum when I saw a tall, thin man in a corner of the court who kept on calling an imaginary dog. He was crying in a soft, tender voice: "Cocotte! Come here, Cocotte, my beauty!" and slapping his thigh as one does when calling an animal. I asked the physician, "Who is that man?" He answered: "Oh! he is not at all interesting. He is a coachman named Francois, who became insane after drowning his dog."

I insisted: "Tell me his story. The most simple and humble things are sometimes those which touch our hearts most deeply."

Here is this man's adventure, which was obtained from a friend of his, a groom:

There was a family of rich bourgeois who lived in a suburb of Paris. They had a villa in the middle of a park, at the edge of the Seine. Their coachman was this Francois, a country fellow, somewhat dull, kind-hearted, simple and easy to deceive.

One evening, as he was returning home, a dog began to follow him. At first he paid no attention to it, but the creature's obstinacy at last made him turn round. He looked to see if he knew this dog. No, he had never seen it. It was a female dog and frightfully thin. She was trotting behind him with a mournful and famished look, her tail between her legs, her ears flattened against her head and stopping and starting whenever he did.

He tried to chase this skeleton away and cried:

"Run along! Get out! Kss! kss!" She retreated a few steps, then sat down and waited. And when the coachman started to walk again she followed along behind him.

He pretended to pick up some stones. The animal ran a little farther away, but came back again as soon as the man's back was turned.

Then the coachman Francois took pity on the beast and called her. The dog approached timidly. The man patted her protruding ribs, moved by the beast's misery, and he cried: "Come! come here!" Immediately she began to wag her tail, and, feeling herself taken in, adopted, she began to run along ahead of her new master.

He made her a bed on the straw in the stable, then he ran to the kitchen for some bread. When she had eaten all she could she curled up and went to sleep.

When his employers heard of this the next day they allowed the coachman to keep the animal. It was a good beast, caressing and faithful, intelligent and gentle.

Nevertheless Francois adored Cocotte, and he kept repeating: "That beast is human. She only lacks speech."

He had a magnificent red leather collar made for her which bore these words engraved on a copper plate: "Mademoiselle Cocotte, belonging to the coachman Francois."

She was remarkably prolific and four times a year would give birth to a batch of little animals belonging to every variety of the canine race. Francois would pick out one which he would leave her and then he would unmercifully throw the others into the river. But soon the cook joined her complaints to those of the gardener. She would find dogs under the stove, in the ice box, in the coal bin, and they would steal everything they came across.

Finally the master, tired of complaints, impatiently ordered Francois to get rid of Cocotte. In despair the man tried to give her away. Nobody wanted her. Then he decided to lose her, and he gave her to a teamster, who was to drop her on the other side of Paris, near Joinville-le-Pont.

Cocotte returned the same day. Some decision had to be taken. Five francs was given to a train conductor to take her to Havre. He was to drop her there.

Three days later she returned to the stable, thin, footsore and tired out.

The master took pity on her and let her stay. But other dogs were attracted as before, and one evening, when a big dinner party was on, a stuffed turkey was carried away by one of them right under the cook's nose, and she did not dare to stop him.

This time the master completely lost his temper and said angrily to Francois: "If you don't throw this beast into the water before—to-morrow morning, I'll put you out, do you hear?"

The man was dumbfounded, and he returned to his room to pack his trunk, preferring to leave the place. Then he bethought himself that he could find no other situation as long as he dragged this animal about with him. He thought of his good position, where he was well paid and well fed, and he decided that a dog was really not worth all that. At last he decided to rid himself of Cocotte at daybreak.

He slept badly. He rose at dawn, and taking a strong rope, went to get the dog. She stood up slowly, shook herself, stretched and came to welcome her master.

Then his courage forsook him, and he began to pet her affectionately, stroking her long ears, kissing her muzzle and calling her tender names.

But a neighboring clock struck six. He could no longer hesitate. He opened the door, calling: "Come!" The beast wagged her tail, understanding that she was to be taken out.

They reached the beach, and he chose a place where the water seemed deep. Then he knotted the rope round the leather collar and tied a heavy stone to the other end. He seized Cocotte in his arms and kissed her madly, as though he were taking leave of some human being. He held her to his breast, rocked her and called her "my dear little Cocotte, my sweet little Cocotte," and she grunted with pleasure.

Ten times he tried to throw her into the water and each time he lost courage.

But suddenly he made up his mind and threw her as far from him as he could. At first she tried to swim, as she did when he gave her a bath, but her head, dragged down by the stone, kept going under, and she looked at her master with wild, human glances as she struggled like a drowning person. Then the front part of her body sank, while her hind legs waved wildly out of the water. Finally those also disappeared.

Then, for five minutes, bubbles rose to the surface as though the river were boiling, and Francois, haggard, his heart beating, thought that he saw Cocotte struggling in the mud, and, with the simplicity of a peasant, he kept saying to himself: "What does the poor beast think of me now?"

He almost lost his mind. He was ill for a month and every night he dreamed of his dog. He could feel her licking his hands and hear her barking. It was necessary to call in a physician. At last he recovered, and toward the 2nd of June his employers took him to their estate at Biesard, near Rouen.

There again he was near the Seine. He began to take baths. Each morning he would go down with the groom and they would swim across the river.

One day, as they were disporting themselves in the water, Francois suddenly cried to his companion: "Look what's coming! I'm going to give you a chop!"

It was an enormous, swollen corpse that was floating down with its feet sticking straight up in the air.

Francois swam up to it, still joking: "Whew! it's not fresh. What a catch, old man! It isn't thin, either!" He kept swimming about at a distance from the animal that was in a state of decomposition. Then, suddenly, he was silent and looked at it attentively. This time he came near enough to touch, it. He looked fixedly at the collar, then he stretched out his arm, seized the neck, swung the corpse round and drew it up close to him and read on the copper which had turned green and which still stuck to the discolored leather: "Mademoiselle Cocotte, belonging to the coachman Francois."

The dead dog had come more than a hundred miles to find its master.

He let out a frightful shriek and began to swim for the beach with all his might, still howling; and as soon as he touched land he ran away wildly, stark naked, through the country. He was insane!

THE CORSICAN BANDIT

The road ascended gently through the forest of Aitone. The large pines formed a solemn dome above our heads, and that mysterious sound made by the wind in the trees sounded like the notes of an organ.

After walking for three hours, there was a clearing, and then at intervals an enormous pine umbrella, and then we suddenly came to the edge of the forest, some hundred meters below, the pass leading to the wild valley of Niolo.

On the two projecting heights which commanded a view of this pass, some old trees, grotesquely twisted, seemed to have mounted with painful efforts, like scouts sent in advance of the multitude in the rear. When we turned round, we saw the entire forest stretched beneath our feet, like a gigantic basin of verdure, inclosed by bare rocks whose summits seemed to reach the sky.

We resumed our walk, and, ten minutes later, found ourselves in the pass.

Then I beheld a remarkable landscape. Beyond another forest stretched a valley, but a valley such as I had never seen before; a solitude of stone, ten leagues long, hollowed out between two high mountains, without a field or a tree to be seen. This was the Niolo valley, the fatherland of Corsican liberty, the inaccessible citadel, from which the invaders had never been able to drive out the mountaineers.

My companion said to me: "This is where all our bandits have taken refuge?"

Ere long we were at the further end of this gorge, so wild, so inconceivably beautiful.

Not a blade of grass, not a plant-nothing but granite. As far as our eyes could reach, we saw in front of us a desert of glittering stone, heated like an oven by a burning sun, which seemed to hang for that very purpose right above the gorge. When we raised our eyes towards the crests, we stood dazzled and stupefied by what we saw. They looked like a festoon of coral; all the summits are of porphyry; and the sky overhead was violet, purple, tinged with the coloring of these strange mountains. Lower down, the granite was of scintillating gray, and seemed ground to powder beneath our feet. At our right, along a long and irregular course, roared a tumultuous torrent. And we staggered along under this heat, in this light, in this burning, arid, desolate valley cut by this torrent of turbulent water which seemed to be ever hurrying onward, without fertilizing the rocks, lost in this furnace which greedily drank it up without being saturated or refreshed by it.

But, suddenly, there was visible at our right a little wooden cross sunk in a little heap of stones. A man had been killed there; and I said to my companion.

"Tell me about your bandits."

He replied:

"I knew the most celebrated of them, the terrible St. Lucia. I will tell you his history.

"His father was killed in a quarrel by a young man of the district, it is said; and St. Lucia was left alone with his sister. He was a weak, timid youth, small, often ill, without any energy. He did not proclaim vengeance against the assassin of his father. All his relatives came to see him, and implored of him to avenge his death; he remained deaf to their menaces and their supplications.

"Then, following the old Corsican custom, his sister, in her indignation carried away his black clothes, in order that he might not wear mourning for a dead man who had not been avenged. He was insensible to even this affront, and rather than take down from the rack his father's gun, which was still loaded, he shut himself up, not daring to brave the looks of the young men of the district.

"He seemed to have even forgotten the crime, and lived with his sister in the seclusion of their dwelling.

"But, one day, the man who was suspected of having committed the murder, was about to get married. St. Lucia did not appear to be moved by this news, but, out of sheer bravado, doubtless, the bridegroom, on his way to the church, passed before the house of the two orphans.

"The brother and the sister, at their window, were eating frijoles, when the young man saw the bridal procession going by. Suddenly he began to tremble, rose to his feet without uttering a word, made the sign of the cross, took the gun which was hanging over the fireplace, and went out.

"When he spoke of this later on, he said: 'I don't know what was the matter with me; it was like fire in my blood; I felt that I must do it, that, in spite of everything, I could not resist, and I concealed the gun in a cave on the road to Corte.

"An hour later, he came back, with nothing in his hand, and with his habitual air of sad weariness. His sister believed that there was nothing further in his thoughts.

"But when night fell he disappeared.

"His enemy had, the same evening, to repair to Corte on foot, accompanied by his two groomsmen.

"He was walking along, singing as he went, when St. Lucia stood before him, and looking straight in the murderer's face, exclaimed: 'Now is the time!' and shot him point-blank in the chest.

"One of the men fled; the other stared at, the young man, saying:

"'What have you done, St. Lucia?' and he was about to hasten to Corte for help, when St. Lucia said in a stern tone:

"'If you move another step, I'll shoot you in the leg.'

"The other, aware of his timidity hitherto, replied: 'You would not dare to do it!' and was hurrying off when he fell instantaneously, his thigh shattered by a bullet.

"And St. Lucia, coming over to where he lay, said:

"'I am going to look at your wound; if it is not serious, I'll leave you there; if it is mortal I'll finish you off.'

"He inspected the wound, considered it mortal, and slowly reloading his gun, told the wounded man to say a prayer, and shot him through the head.

"Next day he was in the mountains.

"And do you know what this St. Lucia did after this?

"All his family were arrested by the gendarmes. His uncle, the cure, who was suspected of having incited him to this deed of vengeance, was himself put in prison, and accused by the dead man's relatives. But he escaped, took a gun in his turn, and went to join his nephew in the brush.

"Next, St. Lucia killed, one after the other, his uncle's accusers, and tore out their eyes to teach the others never to state what they had seen with their eyes.

"He killed all the relatives, all the connections of his enemy's family. He slew during his life fourteen gendarmes, burned down the houses of his adversaries, and was, up to the day of his death, the most terrible of all the bandits whose memory we have preserved."

The sun disappeared behind Monte Cinto and the tall shadow of the granite mountain went to sleep on the granite of the valley. We quickened our pace in order to reach before night the little village of Albertaccio, nothing but a pile of stones welded into the stone flanks of a wild gorge. And I said as I thought of the bandit:

"What a terrible custom your vendetta is!"

My companion answered with an air of resignation:

"What would you have? A man must do his duty!"

THE GRAVE

The seventeenth of July, one thousand eight hundred and eighty-three, at half-past two in the morning, the watchman in the cemetery of Besiers, who lived in a small cottage on the edge of this field of the dead, was awakened by the barking of his dog, which was shut up in the kitchen.

Going down quickly, he saw the animal sniffing at the crack of the door and barking furiously, as if some tramp had been sneaking about the house. The keeper, Vincent, therefore took his gun and went out.

His dog, preceding him, at once ran in the direction of the Avenue General Bonnet, stopping short at the monument of Madame Tomoiseau.

The keeper, advancing cautiously, soon saw a faint light on the side of the Avenue Malenvers, and stealing in among the graves, he came upon a horrible act of profanation.

A man had dug up the coffin of a young woman who had been buried the evening before and was dragging the corpse out of it.

A small dark lantern, standing on a pile of earth, lighted up this hideous scene.

Vincent sprang upon the wretch, threw him to the ground, bound his hands and took him to the police station.

It was a young, wealthy and respected lawyer in town, named Courbataille.

He was brought into court. The public prosecutor opened the case by referring to the monstrous deeds of the Sergeant Bertrand.

A wave of indignation swept over the courtroom. When the magistrate sat down the crowd assembled cried: "Death! death!" With difficulty the presiding judge established silence.

Then he said gravely:

"Defendant, what have you to say in your defense?"

Courbataille, who had refused counsel, rose. He was a handsome fellow, tall, brown, with a frank face, energetic manner and a fearless eye.

Paying no attention to the whistlings in the room, he began to speak in a voice that was low and veiled at first, but that grew more firm as he proceeded.

"Monsieur le President, gentlemen of the jury: I have very little to say. The woman whose grave I violated was my sweetheart. I loved her.

"I loved her, not with a sensual love and not with mere tenderness of heart and soul, but with an absolute, complete love, with an overpowering passion.

"Hear me:

"When I met her for the first time I felt a strange sensation. It was not astonishment nor admiration, nor yet that which is called love at first sight, but a feeling of delicious well-being, as if I had been plunged into a warm bath. Her gestures seduced me, her voice enchanted me, and it was with infinite pleasure that I looked upon her person. It seemed to me as if I had seen her before and as if I had known her a long time. She had within her something of my spirit.

"She seemed to me like an answer to a cry uttered by my soul, to that vague and unceasing cry with which we call upon Hope during our whole life.

"When I knew her a little better, the mere thought of seeing her again filled me with exquisite and profound uneasiness; the touch of her hand in mine was more delightful to me than anything that I had imagined; her smile filled me with a mad joy, with the desire to run, to dance, to fling myself upon the ground.

"So we became lovers.

"Yes, more than that: she was my very life. I looked for nothing further on earth, and had no further desires. I longed for nothing further.

"One evening, when we had gone on a somewhat long walk by the river, we were overtaken by the rain, and she caught cold. It developed into pneumonia the next day, and a week later she was dead.

"During the hours of her suffering astonishment and consternation prevented my understanding and reflecting upon it, but when she was dead I was so overwhelmed by blank despair that I had no thoughts left. I wept.

"During all the horrible details of the interment my keen and wild grief was like a madness, a kind of sensual, physical grief.

"Then when she was gone, when she was under the earth, my mind at once found itself again, and I passed through a series of moral sufferings so terrible that even the love she had vouchsafed to me was dear at that price.

"Then the fixed idea came to me: I shall not see her again.

"When one dwells on this thought for a whole day one feels as if he were going mad. Just think of it! There is a woman whom you adore, a unique woman, for in the whole universe there is not a second one like her. This woman has given herself to you and has created with you the mysterious union that is called Love. Her eye seems to you more vast than space, more charming than the world, that clear eye smiling with her tenderness. This woman loves you. When she speaks to you her voice floods you with joy.

"And suddenly she disappears! Think of it! She disappears, not only for you, but forever. She is dead. Do you understand what that means? Never, never, never, not anywhere will she exist any more. Nevermore will that eye look upon anything again; nevermore will that voice, nor any voice like it, utter a word in the same way as she uttered it.

"Nevermore will a face be born that is like hers. Never, never! The molds of statues are kept; casts are kept by which one can make objects with the same outlines and forms. But that one body and that one face will never more be born again upon the earth. And yet millions and millions of creatures will be born, and more than that, and this one woman will not reappear among all the women of the future. Is it possible? It drives one mad to think of it.

"She lived for twenty-years, not more, and she has disappeared forever, forever, forever! She thought, she smiled, she loved me. And now nothing! The flies that die in the autumn are as much as we are in this world. And now nothing! And I thought that her body, her fresh body, so warm, so sweet, so white, so lovely, would rot down there in that box under the earth. And her soul, her thought, her love—where is it?

"Not to see her again! The idea of this decomposing body, that I might yet recognize, haunted me. I wanted to look at it once more.

"I went out with a spade, a lantern and a hammer; I jumped over the cemetery wall and I found the grave, which had not yet been closed entirely; I uncovered the coffin and took up a board. An abominable odor, the stench of putrefaction, greeted my nostrils. Oh, her bed perfumed with orris!

"Yet I opened the coffin, and, holding my lighted lantern down into it I saw her. Her face was blue, swollen, frightful. A black liquid had oozed out of her mouth.

"She! That was she! Horror seized me. But I stretched out my arm to draw this monstrous face toward me. And then I was caught.

"All night I have retained the foul odor of this putrid body, the odor of my well beloved, as one retains the perfume of a woman after a love embrace.

"Do with me what you will."

A strange silence seemed to oppress the room. They seemed to be waiting for something more. The jury retired to deliberate.

When they came back a few minutes later the accused showed no fear and did not even seem to think.

The president announced with the usual formalities that his judges declared him to be not guilty.

He did not move and the room applauded.

The Grave appeared in Gil Blas, July 29, 1883, under the signature of "Maufrigneuse."

Note from the Editor

Odin's Library Classics strives to bring you unedited and unabridged works of classical literature. As such, this is the complete and unabridged version of the original English text unless noted. In some instances, obvious typographical errors have been corrected. This is done to preserve the original text as much as possible. The English language has evolved since the writing and some of the words appear in their original form, or at least the most commonly used form at the time. This is done to protect the original intent of the author. If at any time you are unsure of the meaning of a word, please do your research on the etymology of that word. It is important to preserve the history of the English language.

Taylor Anderson